celebrations

> *"Sing praises to God, sing praises:*
> *Sing praises to our King, sing praises."*
>
> **PSALM 47:6**

celebrations of praise

365 ways

TO FILL EACH DAY WITH MEANINGFUL MOMENTS

DIANA LÉGERE

ARABELLE PUBLISHING, LLC
CHESTERFIELD, VA

Arabelle Publishing
PO Box 2841
Chesterfield, VA 23832
arabellepublishing.com

Unless otherwise noted, Scripture is taken from the New King James Version®. Copyright © 1982 by Thomas Nelson. Used by permission. All rights reserved.

Cover design: Julie Basinski
Cover photo © Can Stock Photo, Inc.
Saucer Magnolia Tree (photo pg 54) © 2020 by Diana LéGere
Interior Design: Julie Basinski and Lance Buckley

ISBN (978-0-9979126-4-7)
Library of Congress Control Number: 2019957691
Subjects: Christian Living / Devotional / Journal

Printed in the USA

"
_____

"Shout for joy to the Lord, all the earth.
Worship the Lord with gladness;
come before Him with joyful songs.
Know that the Lord is God.
He made us, and we are His;
we are His people, the sheep of His pasture.
Enter His gates with thanksgiving
and His courts with praise;
give thanks to Him and praise His name.
For the Lord is good and His love endures forever;
His faithfulness continues through all generations."

PSALM 100 (NIV)

FOR MY SISTER

live in each season as it passes;
**BREATHE THE AIR, DRINK THE DRINK,
TASTE THE FRUIT AND DESIGN YOURSELF
TO THE INFLUENCES OF THE EARTH."**

HENRY DAVIS THOREAU

introduction

Do you look for reasons to celebrate? Holidays, birthdays, and milestones are the basis for life celebrations. But as I get older, I'm realizing that my best moments have not been marked by a historic event that blasted like a marching band in the annual Christmas parade. Rather, it was a small memorable moment that whispered soothing love to my heart, and put a smile on my face years later.

Every day should be a celebration. And it's the merriments of gratitude throughout the week that make a cherished life. In these moments, we realize that blessings flow from our Creator. Not boxed gifts and glitzy packaging, but the gift of time shared with those we care about. Moments of joy that expand our heart, allowing us to preserve a tiny slice of history to relive again and again. Gratitude teaches us that celebrating life is an art and an attitude of the heart.

This book is about celebrating your year ahead. You're about to become more aware and learn to appreciate special moments and people that God gifts you with each day. Whether you bought this book in January or August, start where you are. The book is set up to reflect four seasons. Each season starts with a devotion, followed by an intro to define that month's theme. There are sections for journaling and an ongoing list of activities. Enjoy the activities outlined for that month. Many

are simple and require little preparation other than your participation. Others need time and money. Engage in the activities that inspire you. Complete them in order or skip around. If an activity doesn't interest you, swap it out with one of your own. There are bonus prompts at the back of this book and blank pages for you to capture the memorable moments you created on your own. Many of the activities you'll enjoy again and may even make them a permanent part of your celebrating repertoire. Whatever you do, revel in each day with thanks as you unearth special moments worthy of praise. As you do, your senses will open to the world around you.

Each day, engage for 30 minutes to discover something new. As you do this, you'll look forward to the celebrations that lie ahead whether a couple hours or an entire afternoon. You may decide a decadent weekend is in order. The way you celebrate is up to you but enjoy each day and do at least one thing to rejoice in life.

Italians have a great saying, "Dolce far niente," which means "the sweetness of doing nothing." Nothing moments aren't about being lazy but enjoying every day. Appreciating hard work and celebrating downtime. Taking pleasure in simple things like relaxing on a lawn chair and watching nature, or taking a walk on a crisp, fall day. Or making a special meal and taking the time to savor every bite.

So, in the spirit of celebration, Alla Tua dolce vita – to your sweet life!

january

> "*Take the first step in faith.*
> *You don't have to see the whole staircase,*
> *just take the first step.*"
>
> **MARTIN LUTHER KING JR.**

anuary might be the best month of the year. After all the festivities of the holiday season, you're ready to wind down and take advantage of this season's natural push toward hibernation. It's time to relax and restore.

It's time to start anew with a clean slate. Whether health, finance, or love …. refuse to live in the past and look toward a brand-new future. The good news is that it's your story and you're the author.

Have you thought about what makes a happy day? Writer Denis Waitley says "Happiness cannot be traveled to, owned, earned, worn, or consumed. Happiness is the spiritual experience of living every minute with love, grace, and gratitude."

January is a good time to get personal and learn how you can experience all the moments of this year with a thankful heart.

As you go through the activities of this month, you will experience more joy as you see the small moments as treasures. Whether it's giving back or carving out time to enjoy a not-so-guilty pleasure, January is all about creating a fresh start. If you think of your years as books of your life, January is the first chapter, and your story is about to be written.

What are you excited about for the future? Explore the daily activities and watch your senses come alive. I believe you will feel blessed and happier than you were before you started. Begin and end each day with gratitude. Give thanks to God. In turn, this is a gift you give yourself that will spill over onto everyone you connect with. The Lord is good.

celebrate
JANUARY

1. **Create a time capsule to celebrate yearly successes**.
As you are boxing up December decorations, why not pack up a year of success to look back on next year. Pick a container that appeals to you but be sure it's sturdy and will withstand years of sifting through it as you celebrate these memories each holiday season. Every January, add to the box. Think about the events of the past year. Which ones brought the most joy to your life? Put a memory in your "time capsule." You might add souvenirs, photos…anything that celebrates happy times. Give thanks to a good year gone by. Each December when you decorate the tree you'll be able to celebrate all the blessings you've been given throughout the years. No matter what has happened, life is intertwined with blessings. When we focus on these things, we see the beauty despite the ashes of our mistakes and misfortunes.

2. **Start a Vision Journal.**
This is a modern "bucket list" where you add key phrases, images, and anything that appeals to you. Make it personal, targeting the goals and plans you want to focus on this year. A vision journal will bring clarity and purpose to your life. As you create a plan for your goals, the journal will keep you laser focused and help you break "Big-Foot" goals into workable, bite size action steps. Dare to declare the intention of working toward a goal and you will achieve it one step at a time as you become accountable and the goal becomes real to you. Chart your progress in your journal with daily, weekly, or monthly milestone moments. Do what works for you. Throughout this book we will create at least one monthly prompt to keep you focused on your dreams. What are you dreaming about?

3. De-clutter.

It might be your car, a closet, or a purse. Too much junk makes it difficult to concentrate, which leads to stress. Hanging on to too many things of the past will keep you stuck there. I'm wondering why I keep a tank top from 1973. I wore it for years when it was no longer cool, but finally retired it to a little box where it now lives in a larger box of cherished keepsakes. Clear out the things that no longer serve a purpose to make room for something new that will enhance your life. To celebrate your success of becoming more organized, buy something new to fill the space you've just created.

4. Create a Zen Zone.

Is there a favorite spot in your home free of stress? Claim a space or enhance a room as your haven for relaxation and soul repair. Enjoy this space for Bible reading, meditation, and prayer or journaling.

5. Celebrate becoming more mindful – think yourself happy.

Write down three things that make you feel happy and schedule a time to enjoy each item on the list during this month. Happiness is a choice. It does not depend on your wealth, circumstances, or the possessions you own. Happy people know that they are blessed despite setbacks and refuse to focus on their limitations. No matter how challenging life is for you, someone has experienced a greater trial. Rather than focus on the negative, smile and take time out for the things that bring happiness to your life. "...count it all joy when you fall into trials..."

6. Celebrate someone *just because.*

Who do you appreciate today that may not know it? Take the time to buy a special gift, wrap it beautifully, and present it to someone you appreciate. If you can't visit them, why not pop on Zoom with a surprise visit and tell them how much they mean to you. Celebrate someone you love.

7. Take pleasure in Aromatherapy.

Did you know that essential oils can improve psychological and physical wellness? Derived from plants, these glorious oils can promote health in your body, mind, and spirit. According to OrganicFacts.net, essential oils relieve stress, boost memory, increase energy levels, speed up healing, regulate sleep, and can even reduce headaches. Due to the variance in oil quality, it's best to do your homework when exploring essential oil options. Two common oils include, peppermint to relieve mental fatigue and lavender for relaxation.

8. Celebrate by laughing out loud.

Watch a favorite comedy. We all have that movie in our collection that no matter how often we watch it, time and again, we laugh out loud. But, don't stop with a movie. Look for ways to find the humor in everything and especially, learn to laugh at yourself. Don't take yourself so seriously. According to the Mayo Clinic laughter releases stress, and long-term, may improve your immune system. Laughing causes your body to release natural painkillers, and improves your mood, so you feel happier. The laughter online university stated that laughing allows your diaphragm to become a powerful pump for your lymphatic circulation, which helps the lymph nodes to clean and filter the fluid running through your body. Watching a one-hour comedy can increase the number of T-Cells, Helper T-Cells, and Natural Killer Cells. Laughter may be the best medicine. Celebrate by finding ways to incorporate things into your life that burst with joy and respond with laughter.

9. journal it!

Add a humor page to your vision journal. Collect images that make you smile. List the humorous events of your life, jokes and other things that make you laugh. Spend time with people that help you to focus on the funny side of life. Laughter can help you live a longer, healthier life.

10. gratitude check:

List 5 people you are grateful for. Celebrate gratitude by saying thank you more often. Think about it each day and remember to say thank you to all the people who help you.

"Then our mouth was filled with laughter,
and our tongue was singing."

PSALM 126:2

11. **Give thanks for your daily bread.**

Participate in a local food drive or go shopping for a needy family in your church or neighborhood.

12. **Celebrate history.**

Prepare a meal passed down from a grandparent or relative. Take time to look up a few facts about the origin of the recipe and country it comes from.

13. **Celebrate Hot Toddy Day.**

January is also National Hot Tea month, so if you prefer a non-alcoholic hot beverage, there are many delicious teas to choose from. Take the time to prepare your special mug. Sit in your Zen Zone or favorite chair and savor every sip. Experience the flavor and the warmth. Relax and appreciate time to be still.

14. **Go to the library or a bookstore and select a book to read.**

For some of us it's easy, and for others, you may not have read a book in years. Give yourself a few hours a week to sink into a comfy chair and transport your mind into another dimension. Reading is a vacation for your soul. If you prefer, you can check out an audio book.

15. **Check out Pinterest inspirational quotes and choose five that encourage you.**

Write inspirational quotes on index cards (or include a new page in your vision journal) and read them each day when you wake up. As you go through the month, add quotes to your collection. Stay positive. "As a man thinks, so he is." Renew your mind daily.

appreciate the gift of
SOLITUDE

Winter is the season of serenity. The world is changing, yet calm and unhurried. God intended us to enjoy all seasons, each with a different purpose, and beauty of its own. If our dream is to escape winter and board a rocket into spring, not only would we lack an appreciation for warmer months, but if we aren't a skier, snow boarder, or an ice-skating queen, winter would be dreadful. I don't know about you, but my scarf and mittens would remain packed in my closet. I'd busy myself with paper chains hoping to rush through the season, impatiently tearing off the rings and anxiously counting the days. I have learned all too well, in wanting to be somewhere else, life becomes unbearable. They say bloom where you are planted. Yes, even in winter.

Join me and experience all the splendor of this season sparkling white season. Your heart will come alive with expectation and wonder. Explore the nuances; the sounds, tastes, and the smells. Enjoy winter engaged.

Have you ever walked along on a winter day and noticed the trees? Deciduous trees shed all their leaves for the winter. The shedding process helps them to conserve energy to survive the harsh winter conditions. What winter does for trees is also good advice for people.

Jeffrey McDaniel says, "trees are expert in letting things go." Leaves just release and drop. The tree relaxes and remains in a resting phase until spring returns. I find it difficult to release something and wait around for the results. I like to hang on tight until you give me the exchange.

Too often, I'm an expert on trying to "make it happen." Could we learn to enter the winter season for that same purpose? Preparing our hearts to release what may have outgrown our life. Let it go, then simply rest and wait for spring. As we meditate on what we're thankful for, we must not forget that as the trees drop their leaves, it may also be time for us to let go. Is there someone or something in your life that no longer serves who you are emotionally or spiritually? Do you maintain a schedule that no longer serves a purpose? Are you doing things that are no longer necessary? There are seasons for everything; people, places, and purpose.

Letting go is hard when we are in control, but when we give it to God, it's easy. He promises a light yoke. It may not be a person, place, or thing you must let go. Maybe it's hurt, fear, bad habits, or failures and regrets. Whatever it is, let it drop. Sometimes we must let go of even good things to make room for the great things. With gratitude, appreciate everything, but also accept that you may make mistakes.

> *"Be still, and know that I am God;*
> *I will be exalted among the nations,*
> *I will be exalted in the earth!*
> *The LORD of hosts is with us;*
> *The God of Jacob is our refuge."*
>
> **PSALM 46:10-11**

16. **Celebrate friendship and write a letter to an old friend.**

You can buy fancy stationery, or if you're crafty, you might enjoy making a special card. You'll find all the supplies you need at a local craft store. We all have that person we've wanted to connect with but too often make excuses. Life has a way of keeping us busy, and before we know it, it's too late. Say the things you want to say while you can.

17. **Take a winter walk on a sunny afternoon.**

Sun provides us with a happy hormone called Serotonin which is much needed in the winter. Savor the fact that the shortest day of the year left us in December. Each day is a little longer in January, but there's still a long way to reach the longest day in June. So, why rush it? Enjoy the shorter days and leisurely pace of this relaxing winter season. January's gift is downtime, guilt-free.

18. Celebrate your positive achievements.

Write down your mistakes of the last year and burn them. Now make a list of all the successes you had last year. Focus on the positive. Keep adding to the list of positive things in your life.

19. Forgive.

Make this next year a year of mercy. Forgiveness does not mean you agree with what the person has done, nor does it say you are accepting it. Forgiveness is allowing yourself to release that person, so you are not wasting negative energy harboring resentment. It allows you to move on.

20. Engage in a smile project.

Smiling can improve your mood so why not do it more and help people to smile. Start an experiment. Track how often you smile at someone and they smile back. Notice that if you don't smile, they don't. The world mirrors what you give it. If you want to be around happy smiling people, be happy and smile!

21. Celebrate National Popcorn Day with a bag of your favorite popcorn and watch a tearjerker movie.

Studies have proven that crying releases stress. Have you ever noticed you just feel better after a good cry? Crying is a cleansing way to get rid of negative emotions and can heal your heart.

22. Celebrate National Coffee Break Day!

Visit your favorite coffee shop to indulge in your favorite coffee beverage. If you go through the driveway, buy a drink for the person behind you.

23. Indulge in a bubble bath.

This is not just any bubble bath. Fill the tub with soothing bubbles and light scented candles. Play beautiful background music and relax for at least 20 minutes. If you don't already do this, you might make this a weekly celebration. Studies have proven that a 20-minute bath will help you sleep better.

24. Celebrate and enjoy the pleasure of a good sleep.

January is famous for white linen sales. Take advantage of the opportunity to buy new bed linens and pillows for a more restful night sleep. Create a unique bedtime ritual to reward yourself for a day well done. Don't skimp on sleep. According to the National Sleep Foundation, we spend up to a third of our life sleeping. It's no wonder that rest is so vital to our health and wellbeing. The average person age 26 to 64 needs between 7-9 hours of sleep each night. Make this the year to improve your health with a better sleep pattern.

25. **Celebrate National Soup Month and make a pot of soup.**

Get comfortable – put on a pair of fuzzy socks and cozy sweatpants. If you've got the time, why not enjoy delicious soup while watching a movie marathon, music fest, or enjoying a read-athon. There won't be many days in the year you can indulge in this guilty pleasure.

26. Learn something new.

It's time to expand your body, mind, and spirit. Whether you sign up for a full course, take a class, workshop, or buy a book, attempt to explore what you've never tried before. Take the time to study something you've always wanted to learn. The benefits will include boosting confidence and self-esteem, but also, you'll make new friends to enjoy the journey of celebration.

27. Enjoy an old-fashioned "Sunday drive."

In a world where we have zoned out on real life in exchange for cell phones and Instagram posts, these leisurely drives area practically a thing of the past. But it's time to renew your spirit and sense of adventure and enjoy the winter wonderland. Any day will work but be sure it's a nice clear day when the freshly fallen snow is still beautiful to look at, but the roads are plowed and safe to drive on. Something is cleansing about looking at the snow on a bright blue-sky day. My childhood memories include embarking on a drive for the sheer pleasure of enjoying the ride. A drive that did not include cell phones, electronic games, or other toys. Only a car filled with the buzz of the family talking and enjoying time together. So, go ahead! Celebrate the good old days. Go for a drive.

28. Celebrate the art of communication while shopping.

Okay, women know how to shop and have been taking advantage of January sales since the ice age. While you're out, take time to chat with strangers. Studies show that talking to people makes us happier. If you have nothing to buy, window shop but make a few connections. Hone your listening skills and let people tell you their stories.

29. Cut back on annual TV viewing.

If you are plunging into the new year with new projects, this will give you plenty of time for achieving goals. Set a goal and plan. Use the time you would watch television to achieve it!

30. Celebrate National Escape Day! Watch a travel video.

With the cold temps outside you can trick your mind into feeling the sensations of a vacation by watching a travel video. Imagine you are visiting the place. Grab a favorite drink, a snack, and enjoy!

31. Inspire Your Heart With Art Day.

Visit a local art museum. Or, if you're feeling more ambitious, pick up some painting supplies and explore your creative side.

> *"Art washes away from the*
> *soul the dust of everyday life."*
>
> PABLO PICASSO

SHE
Chased her
DREAMS
and she
CAUGHT
them

appreciate the gift of
FLOW

We were made for a purpose. Fearfully and wonderfully made, our job is to figure out what it is and do it. It's the place God made for us to be happy and creative. It's where we can serve others. That center where we feel so comfortable, we aren't trying to be anything other than ourselves.

Oprah Winfrey once said that passion is energy. "Feel the power that comes from focusing on what excites you."

Have you ever been in that sweet spot where time flies, but you are entirely unaware of it? That's called "flow" or "in the zone." We're experiencing peak performance. We're in command. The tasks are effortless.

A zone where we're doing what we are created for. Where our God-given talents and passions lie. If we are not in that place, we're always trying to fit in – somewhere. I've been there. Feeling like a round peg trying to fit into a square. How about you?

What are you passionate about? January is an excellent time to think about your skills and talents. What would you be doing right now if you could have any job in the world? What would you be doing even if you would not be paid?

Give thanks and gratitude that God has allowed you to do many things that will prepare you for your purpose.

MEMORIES I AM GRATEFUL FOR...

february

*"You know you're in love when you don't
want to fall asleep because reality
is finally better than your dreams."*
DR. SEUSS

February is the month of love, but it's not all about hearts and romance. To prepare your heart to love others, you begin by loving yourself. That means all of you; positive traits, strengths, and flaws. Neatly woven together, everything about you makes you one-of-a-kind. That's something worth celebrating! There is no one on earth like you. You were made for a purpose and no one is prepared to do what only you can do. As you think about your loved ones this month, meditate on God's love for you. He has lovingly knit you in your mother's womb, and He knows everything about you from your inner fears to the number of hairs on your head. You were uniquely made for a purpose that only you can do. There is no higher purpose in life than doing that with love.

Last month you relaxed and restored your soul by taking time to think about the year ahead while resting and enjoying the solace of winter. With winter now shifting toward spring, there is still time to enjoy a slower pace, but it's also a great time to love yourself and build the best you.

The Latin word, Februum means purification, which makes February a great month to improve your body, mind, and soul. Get ready to step into spring with a new sense of purpose, vitality, and vision.

Although there may a few cynics complaining about the limbo state of February; not quite spring and not winter, I love February for several reasons. It's the month my first child was born, which was the greatest lovefest of my life. It's the color of red, which is one of my favorite colors. And I love the finicky weather because half warm days are better than all cold days. In Virginia, some days feel like spring. Sure, we still get a few merited snow days in February, but there is great comfort in knowing it is the shortest month of the year, and the third month of winter, which is a wonderful thing if you are eager for spring.

Embrace this month as a time to love yourself. A new you will emerge if you let it.

celebrate
FEBRUARY

32. Enjoy a weekend getaway to a rustic cabin with a fireplace.
Bring your favorite hot chocolate, books, comfy jammies, and whatever you need for an ultra-cozy experience.

33. **February is National Chocolate Lovers Month, so we really can't start the month without paying tribute to this decadent treat.** And there is good news! Did you know that chocolate is one of the healthiest foods? Dark chocolate is an antioxidant-rich superfood, which can improve your health. According to the Healthline, a 100-gram chocolate bar with 85% cocoa contains 11 grams of fiber, potassium, zinc, and selenium. It's also loaded with antioxidants such as polyphenols, flavanols, and catechins. You won't want to overdo it, but eating chocolate in moderation is not only healthy but a well-deserved treat. Buy your favorite chocolate bar today and enjoy!

34. **Start exercising.**
You've enjoyed a month of relaxing with no pressure. Now it's time to get in shape for the summer months ahead. Celebrate your body and treat it well. Join a gym or commit to a regular routine at home. If you're inclined to quit routine weight loss or fitness programs, remember that simple lifestyle changes may be all you need. Keep moving. Cut back on sugar. Eat more whole foods. Start somewhere, but just do it!

35. **Celebrate with silence.**
Clear your mind and recharge by scheduling regular times each day to turn off electronics, silence your phone, and steer clear of your PC or tablet. Listen to the sound of nothing. You'll be surprised at how clarity will replace the ruckus of the day.

36. **Check up on your financial health and wellness.**
Look at your budget and see what areas need tweaking. Are you overspending on frivolous things and missing out on those bigger opportunities to enjoy life? According to the Bureau of Labor Statistics, the average person spends $3,008 per year eating out. What better way could you enjoy three thousand dollars? What can you save today?

FAMILY
is the
anchor
that holds
us through
LIFE'S STORMS

appreciate the gift of
FAMILY

Strong family ties = happiness. There is no better way to celebrate the joys of life than beside family. Intimate bonds can be ties of blood or heart. When our life is rich in human interaction, we feel connected and loved, which increases our overall well-being.

Harvard Health Publishing noted that one benefit of strong relationships is improved health and longevity. When we connect with our family and those we love, the affection exchanged releases a stress reducing hormone called oxytocin that lowers blood pressure and decreases depression. Simple hand holding and hugging also release dopamine and serotonin. Cuddling is good for your health.

Studies have shown that it's not the quantity of relationships, but the quality that matters. Immunity is reduced during hostile disagreements. Toxic relationships can wreak havoc in our health. But in healthy relationships physical affection releases "feel good" hormones. Close-knit families not only increase health but provide emotional support to get through the ups and downs of life. It's never too late to rekindle family ties.

But what if your family is far away? I experienced this after moving across the country, creating a gap between us of over 2,000 miles. As visits became less frequent, that did not change the fondness in my heart for my family. Neighbors and friends soon became my extended family. I realized that the person did not indicate family, it's the closeness of the relationship.

Your family can be blood relatives, neighbors, or church family. Most important is having the comradery and joy of sharing ups and downs of life with people who care about you.

"It is truly wonderful when the people of God live together in peace."
Psalm 133:1 (CEV)

37. *journal it*

Revisit your childhood. What do you remember that you enjoyed as a kid? Even if you have painful memories of your youth, if you dig deep, you can recall a good memory. Think about something you looked forward to. Was it a favorite cereal, penny candy, a song? Was it a person who mentored or encouraged you? Step back for even five minutes and celebrate your childhood. Write 3 positive things you learned as a kid.

38. Celebrate Send A Card To A Friend Day February 7.

Now is the time to let someone special know you care. If you are feeling creative, why not make your own card.

39. Celebrate the outdoors.

Enjoying nature improves focus and concentration. Fresh air improves blood pressure and heart rate. It not only cleans your lungs but also clears your mind to give you more energy and making you feel happier. Even if you step outside for 15 minutes during the day, take time to "smell the roses".

40. Celebrate your mind by exploring new possibilities.

Attend a workshop or take an online class. As of this printing, Open Culture lists 1,300 Free Online courses from top universities, Stanford, Yale, MIT, Berkeley and more. Stanford Online, Harvard Extension, Open Yale Courses, MIT Open Courseware, and UC Berkeley Class Central all offer high quality material. Coursera.org also partners with universities and organizations to provide free online education.

"

*the informality of family life is
a blessed condition that allows us all to become
our best while looking our worst.*

MARGE KENNEDY

EVERY single thing that has ever happened in your life is preparing you for a moment that is yet to come

41. **Love your soul: Meditate.**

There are many ways to meditate. I enjoy meditating on the Word of God, which promises great peace. But, the simple act of being still and enjoying a quiet space does more than bring peace. Stillness calms your mind, and breeds clarity and improved concentration. You'll feel relaxed and rejuvenated, and less likely to be overcome by the stresses of the day.

42. **Give the gift of service.**

Volunteer benefits are endless. You not only help someone in need, but it opens the door for you to make new friends, create lifelong bonds, and socialize more. According to the Corporation for National Community and Service, volunteers get a "helpers high" in exchange for service. Research has proven those who volunteer have lower rates of mortality than those who do not. A sense of purpose has been linked to longevity.

43. **Detox as you move out of the last cold month of the year.**

What must you reduce in your life – food, alcohol, television? Purge old bad habits that might be taking control of you. Not all changes will happen overnight, but take small steps and celebrate your success.

44. **Boost your immune system – Jump on a trampoline!**

Jumping on a trampoline is a fun workout that burns calories, and revs up your metabolism and your immune system. According to living strong.com physical activity on a trampoline can strengthen your lymph and immune system, and triggers removal of toxins in your body.

45. **Recharge your outlook on life.**

Today is a good day to take stock your life. Think about things that have caused you negative emotions. Now list all the positive outcomes that have resulted in these incidents. Everything has a silver lining if you find it. Celebrate that God works all things out for the good of those that love him. Your outlook on life is a choice.

They
laugh at me
because I'am
different.
I laugh at them
because they are
all the same.

appreciate the gift of
AUTHENTICITY

Oprah Winfrey says, "You can run away from yourself for a very long time. You can be married to the wrong person for decades and pretend it's fine. You can fake it doing work you only half care about. You can hide behind accouterments, square footage, and cars. Big-screen TVs and fancy vacations. But you will never get away with being a phony." No one will be more aware of that lie than you.

You deserve to live an authentic life that means living the life you live, on purpose. There are no second chances, folks. You can spend your whole life trying to be like someone else, but you will never be better than second best. Or you can spend your life being the best you can be, as yourself.

What are your passions, beliefs, and desires? Are you living true to yourself or trying to be that person everyone else wants you to be?

> *"We need to find the courage to say NO to the things and people that are not serving us if we want to rediscover ourselves and live our lives with authenticity."*
>
> BARBARA DE ANGELIS

46. **Celebrate and honor those you love on Valentine's Day.**

Make an "I Love You" photo collage that includes all the people you love.

47. **Celebrate Random Acts of Kindness Day – February 17.**
Think of ways you can show love toward others. Who can you bless today? Pay for the person behind you in the fast food window, put a surprise on a neighbor's porch. Whatever you do, be kind.

48. **Take a 20-30-minute power nap.**

According to Web MD, power napping can recharge you. Experts say that enjoying the pleasure of daytime naps can combat sleep deprivation. Just as our toddlers lay down for an hour in the afternoon, adults can benefit from a similar routine. A 30-minute nap between 1:00 PM and 3:00 PM can reduce stress, boost memory and enhance creativity.

49. **Treat Yourself Day.**
Buy yourself one quality item you want but don't need. The gift you give yourself can be material or a simple activity. The point is to treat yourself with something special today. We all put ourselves on the back burner. Not today. It's your day. What do you really want?

50. *journal it!*
Start each day focused on love. Remember that God loves you, and in return, you may enjoy others. Meditate on how God shows his love for you. Personalize your journal and create a "love" page and write at least 5 things in it each day that starts with "I love."

51. **Sit quietly in a dark room lit with only candles.**
Candlelight's calming effect reduces stress. Therapists have known for centuries the soothing, healing properties of candlelight. The ambiance creates a soft cozy feel to any room. Candles infused with essential oils will provide a greater experience as you will reap the rewards ranging from relaxation to a boost of energy.

52. **Express appreciation and love by writing 5 thank you notes.**

Thank you notes are a great way to thank the giver but also an opportunity for you to use encouraging words to uplift, someone.

53. **Celebrate dance.**

Grab a BFF (or do it alone) and have a dance party. Play some of your favorite music and dance. Beatles and Beach Boys. My favorite is Get Happy. Who could hear that and not feel better? Dancing is emotionally therapeutic. According to mentalhealthscreening. org, Dancing improves your heart health, overall muscle strength, balance and coordination, and reduces depression. Research has proven that girls who took dance classes improved their mental health and reported a boost in their mood. These positive effects lasted up to eight months after the dance classes ended. What would happen if you initiated a 4-minute "get happy" break at work?

54. **Designate an afternoon as a Spa Day.**

Go solo or invite a couple of girlfriends to join you. Make your own sugar scrub and facial masks.

55. **Host a cooking party.**

Inviting friends to join you in cooking a meal not only makes it easier on you as the party host, but it is a great way to deepen the bonds of friendship. Choose a menu that allows for stations, so each member of the group can oversee a prep task.

56. *gratitude check:*

Write 3 things you love about each of your children and why.

67. **Encouragement is often easier to give to others than ourselves.**

Write yourself a letter of encouragement that builds you up in an area you feel defeated. Place it in another month of this journal and read it again. The more you read it the more encouraged you will feel.

58. **Celebrate your mind by becoming more mindful.**

This is harder than you think. With so much stimulation coming from all directions, we often sleepwalk through life not even aware of what's happening around us. I know. I've been guilty! Train yourself to be more aware of your surroundings and emotions. Live in the present by paying attention to everything around you.

59. Is there someone in your life difficult to love?

Celebrate the love month by showing an act of kindness toward that person. It may be your boss or a coworker, or even someone in your family.

57. Enjoy an evening bonfire with friends.

Hanging with your friends is always fun. Add a fireplace or the flicker of candlelight and we have an intimate get-together. Step outside and make a bonfire and it's a celebration to remember for years. A crackling fire, s'mores, roasted dogs and drinks make a stress-free night of fun that has virtually no clean up or prep work. Add campfire games and laughter and it's all you need to create a memory.

> *"Two are better than one, because they have a good reward for their labor. For if they fall, one will lift up his companion."*

ECCLESIASTES 4:9-10

appreciate the gift of
FRIENDSHIP

Friendship is one of the greatest gifts we can give or receive. According to the Mayo Clinic, friendships have a major impact on our health and well-being. Friendships not only increase our sense of belonging and purpose, but they improve our confidence and self-worth.

We all want to be known. That special person who knows our secrets and likes us anyway. Our genuine unmasked self without walls. We can tell them where we've been, and they get it. We can show them where we live, and they are happy to join us there whether it's a studio or a mansion. They accept what we've grown into and encourage us to continue growing even if it means they might sometimes tag behind. It's a safe place with mutual shared experiences. No expectations. Pure acceptance and love.

C.S. Lewis said that friendship is born at that moment when one person says to another: 'What? You too? I thought I was the only one.'

We're all looking for ourselves. But to be a friend we must put ourselves aside. We must first be a friend. Kindness counts, for whatever we give we will receive. Be a good listener and offer verbal cues to let the other person know you are engaged and present with them. Most important, connect on an intimate level by sharing your own private thoughts and experiences. Be available.

"The glory of friendship is not the outstretched hand, not the kindly smile, nor the joy of companionship. It is the spiritual inspiration that comes to one when you discover that someone else believes in you and is willing to trust you with a friendship." Ralph Waldo Emerson

Are you ready? Gift wrap a friendship and give it to someone today. Appreciate the Gift of friendship.

MEMORIES I AM GRATEFUL FOR...

MEMORIES I AM GRATEFUL FOR...

it is spring again.
the earth is like a child
that knows poems by heart.

RAINER MARIA RILKE

Spring

We've waited, and it's finally here. Spring always comes and once again, hope is rekindled. After surviving a harsh winter, a promise of more light and a sigh of relief. Spring is all about renewal and splendor. Brilliant sunshine radiates against the backdrop of explosive color, and the glorious splendor of God's majesty is revealed. Spring sings to us the power of God's awesome works and celebrates the Lord's abundant goodness. An appetizer of what is yet to come. Opulence comes alive and lets us peek into heavenly realms.

As the earth renews, this is also a time for you to renew your mind, body, and spirit to continue moving forward on the best journey life has for you. Commit to a brand new you.

Give yourself a fresh start by casting out negative thoughts and emotions and embrace this season with positivity and optimism. Spring has a way of compelling us to enter this new season with confidence. Hope has awakened and is alive with wonder.

> *"Look around you: Winter is over;*
> *the winter rains are over, gone!*
> *Spring flowers are in blossom all over.*
> *The whole world's a choir - and singing!*
> *Spring warblers are filling the forest with sweet arpeggios.*
> *Lilacs are exuberantly purple and perfumed, and*
> *cherry trees fragrant with blossoms. Oh, get up, dear*
> *friend, my fair and beautiful lover - come to me!"*
>
> SONG OF SOLOMON 2:11-13 (MSG)

march

> "*It was one of those March days when the
> sun shines hot and the wind blows cold;
> When it is summer in the light
> and winter in the shade.*"

CHARLES DICKENS

Buttercups, spring azaleas, and cherry blossoms are hallmarks of March. Perennial gardens spiral to life with daffodils and tulips. Virginia is one of my favorite places to enjoy spring. Nothing compares to the buds and flowers that suddenly pop up everywhere! Fragrant cherry blossoms, which peak at the end of March, are a major attraction in Washington DC. From the Japanese cherry blossoms to the dogwood trees and stunning azalea bushes, God's glory is alive with color, fresh scents, and perpetual beauty. One of my favorite flowering trees is the saucer magnolia. The delicate pink dancing blooms remind me of a choir, and the heavens are calling us to join the most exquisite party. It's time to awaken from our winter slumber as we're energized by the warm breeze, spring colors, and fragrant scents. The alarm clock is buzzing. I don't know about you, but this time of year I'm eager to get up! I'm excited to make a bouquet of my favorite flowers. What are your favorite spring blooms?

celebrate
MARCH

61. Celebrate sunshine.

Nothing is more tranquil than feeling the warmth of the sun on your shoulders and embracing the calm of a quiet spring day. You might lie in a hammock and take a nap. Or sit on a comfy chair and read a book. Or perhaps the kid in you will emerge, and you'll blow bubbles by yourself or with a friend.

62. **Celebrate the fragrance of spring.**

Open the windows and let the fresh air in. Take a walk outside and notice the scents of the spring blossoms or the fresh cut grass.

63. **Choose happiness.**

Now is the time to let things go that have not brought joy into your life. Renew your spirit by letting go of the old and bringing something new into your life. What will it be?

64. **Clean your car inside and out.**

You will experience a feeling of peace and be energized for some travel and vacation days that lie ahead. To reward yourself, take a short drive and explore new territory.

65. **Clean up emotional clutter holding you back.**

Walt Disney said, "The way you get started is to quit talking and start doing." Are there decisions you have been putting off? Firmly commit to decide today, the move forward with the action to make your goals and dreams a reality.

66. *journal it!*

Write about 3 life lessons you've learned in your lifetime.

67. *gratitude check:*

Think positive. Write 5 positive I AM statements about yourself.

68. **Celebrate music.**

Select music you usually would not listen to. If you are rarely a serious music fan, classical tunes are a beautiful place to begin. Vivaldi's Four Seasons is a lively selection and one of my favorites. Lay back close your eyes and listen to the instruments. Relax and let the music flow through your body.

69. **Celebrate St. Patrick's Day, March 17.**

Prepare an authentic Irish meal.

70. **Buy your favorite fresh flowers and a pretty vase and spend time arranging a lively bouquet.**

Air cleaning flowering plants include Mums and Gerber Daisies. For cut flowers enjoy Freesia, Lilacs, Gardenias, Roses, Asian and Stargazer Lilies, Jasmine, and Hyacinth which all have beautiful fragrances. The health benefits of flowers in your space include reduced blood pressure and an overall positive impact on your emotional health and wellbeing.

71. **Boost your creativity and decrease anxiety by feeding the ducks.**

Be kind and skip the bread. Healthier choices for birds include birdseed, corn or peas, popped corn, or oats.

72. **Restore your soul beside still waters.**

Skip rocks on a pond. Or maybe just dip your toes in the water. Our bodies are 65-70% water so it seems natural why we are pulled to the water's edge. Studies have shown those who live by the ocean or other body of water feel less stress. Even having a small fountain on your desk can bring positive effects. Sights and sounds of water quiet the brain and bring you to a meditative state.

73. **Celebrate spring.**

Buy organic and locally grown foods at a Farmer's Market.

74. **Rid yourself of unfinished projects.**

Why are these projects undone? Are they projects that no longer serve your life? Can you realign them to better suit your life? It's okay to cross them off your list. But if procrastination has stood in your way, empower your self-esteem by setting a goal to complete at least one unfinished project. Who knows, you might cross off a few more!

75. *journal it!*

Write down 3 simple pleasures you enjoy. Make time and schedule these things daily or weekly.

appreciate the benefits of
MUSIC

usic can ease pain, produce relaxation, improve sleep, and reduce stress. Studies have shown that stress causes 60% of all illness and disease. According to an article by the Pfizer Medical team (gethealthystayhealthy.com) in studies of people with cancer, listening to music combined with standard care reduced anxiety compared to those who received standard care alone. Additional studies have shown that music has helped people with Alzheimer's recollect seemingly lost memories.

Classical music is uplifting and proven to relieve depression. While listening to music the brain releases dopamine, the "feel good" transmitter

"Praise Him with the sound of the trumpet;
praise Him with the lute and harp!
Praise Him with the timbral and dance;
praise Him with the stringed instruments and flutes!
Praise Him with loud cymbals;
praise Him with clashing cymbals!"

PSALMS 150: 3-5

76. Make a bird feeder.

There are many fun and easy bird feeders you can make. One of the easiest ways to make a bird feeder is to cover an item with peanut butter and roll it in bird seed. Add a ribbon and hang these in the trees around your home. A few items that work well include pine cones, sugar cones, toast, bagels, and even non-edible items work. Try coating a toilet paper roll, small paper plate, or a wooden cut out. After you've set up your feeders, take a few minutes each day to enjoy watching your birds.

77. Take a cooking class.

Sur La Table and Williams Sonoma both offer many hands-on cooking classes. Themes include seasonal cooking, ethnic cuisines, pizza workshops, date nights, and more.

78. Celebrate National Pack Your Lunch Day.

Take your lunch break and enjoy a peaceful picnic in the park.

79. Celebrate a healthy body.

Purge processed foods and commit to eating more whole grains.

80. Get a fresh start with a spring-cleaning ritual.

Be creative and repurpose a few items and rearrange the furniture.

81. Celebrate your body.

Start a simple exercise routine today and make a goal to do it for at least 14 days until it's a habit. It need not be long. Faithfulness matters most.

82. Every moment matters.

Think about an event you have scheduled in your life. It can be a birthday or other anther simple milestone you want to celebrate. Memorable moments are notable and will leave a lasting impression for you and the recipient. How can you make the next ordinary festivity extraordinary? Have fun making it happen.

83. *journal it!*

Write about a time when someone made a day memorable for you.

84. Celebrate song.

Step outside of your comfort zone and get a group together to enjoy a night of Karaoke.

85. Celebrate National Water Day.

Make a conscious effort to drink more water this month. Hydrate yourself with 6-8 glasses and note the difference in how you feel. Every cell, organ and tissue in your body uses water to regulate

86. Celebrate appreciation.

Make a list of three ways you feel people appreciate you. As you move through this season offer feelings of gratitude to others as you acknowledge what you appreciate about them. Add an appreciation page in your vision journal and write down all the people you appreciate each day.

87. Set a date with yourself.

Enjoy an activity alone. With no distractions and conversation, you will absorb yourself completely into the activity.

88. Spring forward.

Do someone a favor. How can you be a blessing today?

89. *journal it!*

Write out your "Bucket List." Explore options with abandon and do not think of the possibilities of the items on your list. Just write. Next, read your list. Put a star next to all the things you could check off this year. Pick one to do first.

90. Celebrate your body.

Start a simple exercise routine today and make a goal to do it for at least 14 days until it's a habit. It need not be long. Faithfulness matters most.

91. *journal it!*

Do you live to work or work to live? Love yourself to find balance in your life. Look at your job as a blessing that provides the resources for you to embrace and enjoy life.

Why do you appreciate your job?

Write in your journal all the benefits of your job.

MEMORIES I AM GRATEFUL FOR...

MEMORIES I AM GRATEFUL FOR...

april

> *"April has put the spirit of youth in everything."*
> **WILLIAM SHAKESPEARE**

Well said. If March was the first day of hope after a long dreary winter, April is the month that finally tells us that hope has arrived and it's time to celebrate and host a party!

Celebrations of Praise is a mindset of accepting each moment of each day as a gift. What better time to put this motto into action as you open the window to spring? As you enjoy April, embrace each day. Time is given to us as a gift from God. Like money management, time management may be even more important.

King Solomon said we should eat every meal as though it were a banquet, celebrate every day as though it were a party, live every day we are married as though we are on our honeymoon, and work every day as though it is our final achievement. Can you imagine how you would feel about life –your life, if you did that?

How many hours a day do we waste each year and at the end of our lives we are wishing we could have just one more day?

"Time cannot be stored or stopped or slowed. Because there is a time limit to everything in this life, each experience is a gift that we have been entrusted with and must not waste." Dr. David Jeremiah.

April reminds me of children frolicking in the fields, free of worry. Childlike laughter echoes through the fields. Wonder and delight permeate the space. This month let your inner child out to explore and savor blessings. Trust God to reveal new possibilities as you grow deeper in His presence and enjoy life as a celebration.

celebrate
APRIL

92. Take a friend to lunch.

Find a cozy spot to enjoy hearty pub food and celebrate a special friendship.

93. Plan a trip.

April is a great month to get deals on travel. Cruises are usually running specials this month. Studies have shown the simple act of planning is almost as fun as going there. Pick up travel brochures, peruse travel sites and let your imagination create the perfect summer escape.

94. Celebrate spring with a backyard family game day.

Bocce ball, corn hole, crochet, volleyball, badminton, or ping pong are all fun outdoor games that are fun for all ages.

95. Go fishing.

96. **Rent paddle boats.**

97. **April showers bring May flowers.**
Take a wanton walk in the rain without an umbrella.

98. **Visit a Farmer's Market and buy a selection of fresh greens and veggies.**
Make a big salad to enjoy throughout the week. Add as many colorful vegetables as in season.

99. **Treat yourself to a big bouquet of your favorite flowers.**
Experience all the sensations of arranging the flowers in a vase.

100. **Celebrate the team!**
Join a baseball team or find one to support.

101. **April 12 is Drop Everything And Read Day.**
Take time to appreciate the quiet of reading a good book.

102. **Celebrate spring by collecting flowers.**
Make a pressed flower collage for your wall or give it as a gift.

103. **Celebrate National Card and Letter Writing Month.**
Write a letter to a friend or relative that lives far away.

104. **Celebrate Color.**
Spend time indulging your creativity by coloring Easter eggs. If you don't eat eggs, give them away as gifts. Fill a small basket with colored eggs and add a note to encourage a neighbor or special friend.

105. **National Stress Awareness Day.**
De-stress with essential oils.

106. *journal it!*
Write about a spring memory shared with your siblings.

107. *gratitude check!*
Experience nature and make a list of all the things you are grateful for in the outdoors.

108. **Buy a small gift for someone you care about.**
Surprise them with the gift and a note; "I was thinking about you."

109. **Soak up sunshine.**
Sit on a park bench and enjoy feeling the warm sunlight.

110. **Explore a botanical garden.**
Watch spring unfold and experience the magic of butterflies.

111. **Celebrate National Bike Day.**
Take a bike ride and enjoy the beautiful scenery along the way. Think about how free you felt as a child riding a bike.

112. **Celebrate peace and tranquility.**
Walk in the woods. Notice everything that surrounds you. The sounds of the birds, whisper of the wind, the colors. Explore and delight in your findings.

113. **Embark on a discovery walk of color.**
Make a list of all the colors you uncover as you walk around your neighborhood. How many colors do you normally take for granted?

114. **April 22 is Earth Day.**
Plan an planting activity to celebrate the earth.

115. **Create a spring project list.**
Beautify your patio or yard by adding flowers or shrubs.

116. **Enjoy a long hot shower.**
When was the last time you were present in the shower? Or is your mind being on a million other tasks ahead? Instead, feel the stream of hot water and enjoy the relaxing heat as it soothes your muscles. Unwind and let stress disappear.

117. *gratitude check:*

Think about all your favorite smells and list them. What is the smell you love the most? Think about how you can incorporate that into your daily routine.

118. Hug a friend day. April 26.

Purposefully hug people today. Studies have shown that hugs can make you happier. Dr. Mercola says that a 20-second hug can reduce the physical effects of stress, including lowering your heart rate and blood pressure.

119. Celebrate National Picnic Day on April 23.

Although picnics have become a beloved American tradition, they were first enjoyed by the French in the 17th century. This favorite Al Fresco Meal – add info

120. Celebrate frugality.

Go thrift store shopping and select an item to repurpose for your home or patio. If you prefer to choose something from your own attic or garage.

121. Watch a sunset.

If you enjoy photography, snap some photos to add to your vision journal.

appreciate the beauty of
NATURE

Unroll the tapestry of nature and reflect on its beauty. See the intricate details of a flower. Have you ever set out to see? With open eyes, explore the wonder of life. Everything is beautiful. Our creator has given us an expression of Himself. Just as our homes reflect our nature by providing a glimpse of who we are to our visitors, so God has done the same in the world in which He made splendor. Absorb the beauty of the world around you. Let God's elements be the forefront of the worldly additions that clutter our vision.

When we see the genuine beauty and absorb it, we reflect it to the world. That which fills us flows out of us. Commit to seeing good in the world.

"Let the Heavens rejoice,
and let the earth be glad;
Let the sea roar, and all its fullness;
Let the field be joyful, and all that is in it.
Then all the trees of the woods will rejoice."

PSALM 96: 11-12

MEMORIES I AM GRATEFUL FOR...

MEMORIES I AM GRATEFUL FOR...

#

> *"My wish is to stay always like this,*
> *living quietly in the corner of nature."*
> CLAUDE MONET

May might be one of the most beautiful months of the year. According to a Gallup Survey from 1960 and through 2005, May has consistently been the favorite month of Americans. Winter is long gone, and spring has arrived, and we are getting ready to transition into summer. There's no chance the weather will take a turn back. We are heading into summer! Everywhere, we see brilliance of color with flowers blooming everywhere. Birds chirping, bees, and butterflies grace our gardens, and the fresh air is exhilarating.

May is the kickoff to summer on Memorial Day when BBQs open and beaches draw crowds. Don't let your excitement for summer fun let this month slip away without appreciating it for what it is. This last month of spring has an enchantment all its own.

"When they are already budding, you see and know for yourselves that summer is near." Luke 21:30

celebrate

MAY

122. **Celebrate Cinco de Mayo on May 5th.**
Why not invite friends to spend time in the kitchen cooking up a Mexican feast?

123. Celebrate efficiency.
Get organized and make a lamented list of essential resources you use regularly. Keep it in a handy place or in the fridge.

124. May Day means celebrating flowers.
Buy a bouquet of flowers and leave them on someone's doorstep.

125. Take a nature walk with a friend.

126. Write a letter to someone who taught you a life lesson.

127. May 6th is National Scrapbooking Day.
Now is a great time to pull out all the shoe boxes of photos and put them in an album. If you have digital photos, Shutterfly is a great resource to create a photo memory book.

128. Taste a new food you've never tried.

129. Meditate in a garden.

130. Visit a museum.

131. Celebrate your mom.
Make her a deck of cards with "52 things I love about you."

132. Kindness matters.
Do a kind gesture for your neighbor.

133. Clean out a closet.
Pack up a donation for the Goodwill.

134. Spring is a great time to renew friendships.
Connect with an old friend.

135. Invite a gal pal to get coffee.
Tell her how much her friendship means to you.

136. Share.
Gather old magazines and bring them to a nursing home.

137. Be thankful.
Often, we go through life receiving many gestures of kindness from others which go unnoticed. Count how often you can take time to say thank you to people for the little things and mean it.

138. Send a gratitude card to a friend or family member.
Let them know that you appreciate them and list what they've done for you.

139. *journal it!*

List 3 things that made you feel happy yesterday. Think about how you can repeat these in the days to come.

140. Simplify.
Is there a routine, daily or weekly that has no real purpose or pleasure? Commit to living purposeful in all your daily routines.

141. Meditate on the gift of today.
God's blessings are everywhere. Look for them and seize the moments.

142. Be appreciative.
Give sincere compliments to everyone today.

143. *journal it!*

Think gratitude. Journal this sentence and fill in your responses. I am fortunate because…

144. Create a short-term goal you wish to accomplish by fall.
Develop a plan and work toward it daily.

145. Designate a Spa Day.
Cosmetics and skin care items go on sale in May in honor of Mother's Day. Buy a few items and pamper yourself.

146. Wrap a thank you gift for someone who has shown you kindness.
It can be something you baked or a gift you bought at the store.

147. *journal it!*

Make a memorable moments list.

148. Bake a batch of cookies.

Share them with your neighbors.

149. Invite a few friends over.

Enjoy a backyard BBQ.

150. *gratitude check:*

What are you grateful for this spring? Make a list of 5 things.

151. Wake up early and enjoy breakfast outside.

Take time to enjoy your meal and experience the pleasures all around you. Hear the music of nature.

MEMORIES I AM GRATEFUL FOR...

MEMORIES I AM GRATEFUL FOR...

"now learn this parable from the fig tre
When its branch has become tender and p
forth leaves, you know that summer is nea

MATHEW 24:32

summer

Cherished moments happen between June Solstice to September Equinox when we appreciate and enjoy the warmest months of the year. The sky is ablaze with sunshine that soaks warmth into our skin. Wedged between delightful sweet mornings and magical nights are sultry days long enough to hug an array of activities from afternoon naps on the hammock to high energy fun on the racetrack. We're bustling from one pleasant activity to the next. It's vacation time whether you are enjoying a staycation, out-of-town trip, or weekly days off from work. Summer is a season best enjoyed with friends and family.

As a kid, I remember frolicking in the fields with my siblings until nearly dark. We traipsed around carrying Maxwell House coffee cans and collected everything from shimmering rocks to baby toads as we walked barefoot through the fields and tree lined trails. We never got sick of the smell of cut grass, steaks sizzling on the grill, or cows.

We cringed at the sound of our mother calling us back once she realized the sunlight was shifting and the house was quiet without us. Our trek back home was slow and half-hearted. If we had our way, we'd spend the entire day outside. To live in the sunshine, swim in the pond, and breath in the clean fresh air.

But all was well. We knew we'd soon be awakened early by the stream of sunshine peeking in our bedroom windows. We loved these days; so long they nearly stretched into each other and sleeping didn't seem to fit our schedule.

For all of us, summertime is like a song we want to dance to on repeat for days. We come alive, yet we have permission to be lazy. It means lying on the grass finding images in the clouds is not a waste of time but a matter of preference. So, what will you do to enjoy this season?

june

> "*Keep your face to the sun
> and you will never see the shadows.*"
>
> **HELEN KELLER**

June is always my favorite month. The days are brighter, and the scents and colors are delicious. For one, it's my birth month. And I enjoy this first month of summer when the weather is still comfortable. Roses are in full bloom. I love the variation of colors and enjoy filling my house with their sweet smell. In June, the fragrant buds of every flower blesses us. I love being awakened by a whiff of Wisteria. Botanical Gardens are exploding with colors, fragrances, bees, and butterflies.

With windows open and curtains blowing, the reminders of my childhood come alive with memories of sunshine, basking in the hot rays, and endless time for play. June reminds me of summer break, and my mind can't help but remember those lazy summers of my youth when I had nothing better to do than bask in the sun for hours. The days spent outdoors, walking along the fields were punctuated with a feeling we were glad to be alive. What do you remember from your childhood summers? Is there something that sparks a memory and takes you back to whimsical days of your youth?

celebrate

JUNE

152. **Celebrate National Camping Month.**
Camp in your backyard. Build a fire and make s'mores as you enjoy a simple night of fun.

153. *gratitude check:*

Think about the happiest days of your life.

What is the common thread in those days?

154. **Treat yourself to a manicure and pedicure.**
Buy a new pair of sandals.

155. Make sun tea.

156. Set up the card table on your patio.
Work on a puzzle while enjoying the fresh air and sunshine.

157. *journal it!*
Make a list of your top 5 strengths. Think about how you can incorporate them into your work and daily routine.

158. Celebrate music.
Blues festivals are everywhere.

159. Celebrate National Best Friends Day – June 8.

160. Celebrate the official start of summer on June 20.
June Solstice is the longest day of the year.

161. Visit a state or National Park.

162. Celebrate National Get Outdoors Day – June 11.
Spend the day at a lake.

163. Fly a kite day!

164. Take a boat ride.

165. Visit an aquarium.

166. Enjoy al fresco dining.
Invite a friend to your favorite outdoor café.

167. Sow seeds.
June is the time to plant your outdoor gardens. Sunflowers, coneflowers, and zinnias are especially rewarding to plant as they take little skill to produce beautiful buds.

168. Take your lunch break outside and enjoy a free outdoor concert.

169. Book a romantic dinner cruise.

170. Enjoy a Sunday Jazz Brunch.

171. Celebrate Father's Day.
Thank your Heavenly Father for all the men who have
blessed your life.

172. Inspire someone –
with words of encouragement and thanks.

173. Celebrate Hospitality.
Enjoy a BBQ dinner with family and friends.

174. *gratitude check:*
Make a gratitude list of 10 reasons you like summer.

175. Go swimming –
or relax by a pool.

176. Enjoy a summer drive to the country.

177. Go to the beach.
Experience the sand between your toes and the soothing sounds of
the waves crashing on the shoreline.

178. Visit a winery.
The views are breathtaking, and the experience is pure indulgence
and relaxation. You'll want to bring your camera.

179. Join a fitness club.
Or sign up for an exercise class. There are specials everywhere.

180. Enjoy a weekday movie.
Many theaters will run specials to entertain kids out of school.

181. Explore your creative side and color.
Adult coloring books are therapeutic and serve as a relaxing
pastime to de-stress from a hectic workday.

MEMORIES I AM GRATEFUL FOR...

MEMORIES I AM GRATEFUL FOR...

july

> "*Enjoy the little things, for one day you may look back and realize they were the big things.*"
>
> ROBERT BRAULT

ULY IS THE SECOND MONTH OF SUMMER AND THE WARMEST MONTH OF THE YEAR, OFTEN called the "dog days" of summer. There's no turning back. Summer is here to stay.

It's the month when we drop all regard to stress by slipping out of our work clothes and chasing our dreams (barefoot) in the sunshine. We indulge in our fascination with sand, outdoor concerts, and enjoy our meals while laying on lush green grass. For 31 days, being lazy is not only allowed, it's respected in July. Take a chill pill, it's time to relax.

The aroma of summer smothers us all month long with lingering smells of grilled beef and chicken, gardenias, and freshly mowed grass. Even the sun smells good. We listen as swarms of bees, birds, and butterflies flutter and buzz by. Sights, sounds, and tastes come alive in July and there is no better time for friends and family to gather.

One of my favorite things about July is eating ice cream for dinner. With the array of street festivals, farmers markets, and other community events, it's acceptable to eat whatever you like for dinner. Stoves are unnecessary in July, which means a lot less dish washing.

July is the freedom month. Freedom from work, excessive protocol in regard to attire, and living each day with abandon. You are free!

Perhaps that's why people laugh more. We celebrate the freedom of our country. We also celebrate our freedom in general. Celebrate July as the month to indulge on life's little pleasures.

celebrate
JULY

182. Let your inner child out.
Celebrate the hottest month of the year with a family squirt gun or water balloon fight.

183. Celebrate National Ice Cream Month.
Treat a friend to a sundae.

184. Treat yourself to a massage.

185. Celebrate July 4th.
Host a traditional holiday cookout for family and friends.

186. **Enjoy a fireworks display.**
Some areas will allow you to host your own fireworks shows in your backyard. Red, white, and blue sparklers are a fun way to enjoy the festivities. Be sure to follow all fire regulations.

187. **Global Forgiveness Day.**
Make a list of all the people you want to forgive. I forgive _____ for. Read your list out loud and burn the list.

188. **Visit the zoo.**

189. **Plan a celestial celebration with an evening of sky watching.**
A few celestial events to look for each month include the Supermoon, Super Blue Moon, Lunar Eclipse, and Meteor Showers.

190. **Celebrate light.**
No enchanted summer evening would be complete without an evening spent with fireflies. These twinkling bugs as winged beetles. There are about 2000 species of fireflies. If you live in the east, you will be lucky to enjoy them. Fireflies in the west do not light.

191. **Tie Dye a shirt.**

192. *gratitude check:*
Make a list of 7 things that make you grateful for summer.

193. **Host a family reunion.**

194. **Make S'mores with a friend.**

195. **Celebrate National Puzzle Day, July 13.**

196. **Prepare a meal or bake cupcakes for a neighbor.**

197. **Host a summer card game night.**
Bunco, Bridge, Rummy, or Poker, whatever you enjoy, relax and play cards.

198. **Praise a stranger.**
Buy a motivational card. Put a note in it and write on the envelope, "This card is for you." Leave it in a random public place, like a park bench, bus seat, restaurant table, etc.

199. **Visit an Audubon Center.**

200. **Buy postcards from your town.**
Mail them to a friend in another state.

201. **Take a hike.**
Visit one of the local parks.

202. *gratitude check:*
Make a Gratitude list of 10 things you like about your home.

203. **Let your inner child out.**
Explore your creativity with finger paints.

204. **Celebrate Summer Leisure day, July 22.**
Buy a hammock and swing on it until you fall asleep.

205. **Enjoy an afternoon in the park.**

206. **Dip your toes in water –**
Go to the beach, lake or community pool

207. *journal it!*
The real excitement in life is the journey speckled with a treasure trove of memories and moments collected along the way. Write about a few of your favorite memories.

208. **Celebrate the kid in you! July 27 is Bugs Bunny's Birthday.**
That's right. When's the last time you watched cartoons?

209. **Explore the sights and sounds of a Jazz Festival.**

210. Let the kid out!

Yes, again. It's summer and time to have fun. Challenge your significant other to an old-fashioned balloon fight.

211. Celebrate positivity.

As we think in our heart we will be. Think happy positive, love, and joyful thoughts into the garden of your mind. Remember that whatever we dwell on gets bigger. We can dwell on the negative in our life, or the positive. Happiness is a choice.

212. Take a ride on a Merry-Go-Round.

MEMORIES I AM GRATEFUL FOR ...

MEMORIES I AM GRATEFUL FOR ...

august

> **"You cannot do a kindness too soon because you never know how soon it will be too late."**
>
> **RALPH WALDO EMERSON**

ugust is the last month of summer where we invariably wind down and try to savor the lazy days of summer if we can. It's also the last month of the season when we will enjoy outdoor activities before the chill of fall sets in.

If you haven't taken a vacation, now is the time. As a child, my favorite vacation memory was on Cape Cod where the beaches were tranquil and less crowded. Plates piled high with seafood and bike rides around the island. What I remember most fondly is the lack of schedules. Time seemed endless.

But teen years and adulthood now seem worlds apart. As I grow older I find it necessary to live more purposely as the gap between free time and work schedules seems to widen each year. Is it just me or do you struggle to find time to relax?

I'm determined this year to treat August a little differently. If that week or two vacation escapes me, at the least I want to appreciate and enjoy my regular days off.

213. Build a campfire and make S'mores.

214. Visit a local Farmer's Market and buy fresh produce.

215. Celebrate Watermelon National Day - August 3

216. *journal it!*

Think about 5 things that make you smile and write them in your vision journal. Clip magazine images of these things to paste into your journal.

217. Celebrate National Sister Day.

If you have no sister, grab a BFF and celebrate the sisterhood you share with your girlfriends. (National Girlfriends Day is August 1.)

218. Celebrate Root Beer Float Day, August 6

219. Try out a new salad recipe and make extra for a neighbor.

220. *gratitude check:*

Make a Gratitude list of 10 things you like about yourself.

221. Buy a book on National Book Lovers Day, August 9

222. Lazy Day, August 10

223. Gather summer clothing for your local Goodwill.

224. Celebrate music.

Thomas Edison invented the phonograph on August 12, 1877. Buy a new CD and spend time quietly listening to music and lyrics. Relax and enjoy!

225. Make homemade lemonade.

Invite a neighbor to enjoy it with you.

226. The 2nd week of August is National Smile Week.

Make a list of activities and things that make you smile. Plan to check off at least one activity each day.

227. Visit a country fair. Be sure to enjoy a bag of cotton candy.

228. *journal it!*

Count how often you can smile in a day. Record in your journal the results and how you felt.

229. Enjoy an old fashioned summer picnic on a blanket.

230. *gratitude check:*

Write 3 abilities you have that you are thankful for and pick one to use to help someone else.

231. **God commanded us to give thanks not only in everything, (1 Thessalonians 5:18) but for everything (Ephesians 5:20).**

What are you thankful for today?

232. **Give yourself a manicure and a hand massage.**

233. **Enjoy a day at the at the lake or community pool.**

234. **Enjoy a scoop of your favorite gelato.**

235. **Celebrate fellowship. Visit a senior.**

236. **Write a thank you letter to someone who has inspired you.**

237. **Visit a pet store and play with the puppies or kittens.**

If you have a pet, buy a special surprise for your little pal. Spending time with animals is scientifically proven to raise endorphins and happiness in people.

238. **Play mini golf.**

239. **Enjoy an outdoor concert.**

240. **August is a great month for shoe sales.**

Go ahead. Buy another pair! Buy one for yourself and another pair to give away.

241. Make a difference in someone's life today.

There is a saying, you might be one person to the world, but you can be the whole world to one person. Instead of thinking about how we cannot help enough, think about what we CAN do! There may be someone right in your neighborhood that has a need you can fill.

Think about three gifts you have received that you are most thankful for and write the givers a thank you note telling them why you cherish their gift.

242. *gratitude check:*

Think about three gifts you have received that you are most thankful for and write the givers a thank you note telling them why you cherish their gift.

243. Go berry picking.

Make a few jars of jam to share with a neighbor.

MEMORIES I AM GRATEFUL FOR...

MEMORIES I AM GRATEFUL FOR...

...and let us not grow weary while doing good, for in due season we shall reap, if we do not lose heart.

GALATIANS 6:9

Fall

sher out summer and marshall in fall. The days are getting shorter and the leaves are changing. Fall turns up the color and there are many ways to enjoy the tapestry of this season. It's no coincidence that the Lord shows off an array of colors that go out in the same powerful display just as it arrived in the spring.

I moved to the west in the fall and I was captivated by the beauty there. The Bible says the works of the Lord are wondrous. As I caught my breath to take in the beauty of the mountains, I saw it like nothing I had ever witnessed. A vision so intense it bought me to tears. Mountains so massive they could swallow an entire city. Yet somehow comforting, surrounding the area like a cozy blanket of protection. Each morning God was saying, open your heart to receive the true gifts of this day. Blessings are in store for you.

Whether you live in the north, south, east or west, God's radiant presence is evident in the rising sun and gentle rays peeking though the trees, the morning dew, sounds of the forest as birds flutter and sing praises to our King. Good morning. Rejoice! This day is for you to have an enjoy. Receive it with gladness.

"This is the day the Lord has made;
we will rejoice and be glad in it."

PSALM 118:24

september

> "*Lots of people want to ride with you in the limo, but what you want is someone who will take the bus with you when the limo breaks down.*"
>
> **OPRAH WINFREY**

s it just me? I'm still clinging to summer. Every year, I go through a brief, but adamant protest phase. As summer transitions into to fall, I refuse to cooperate. Vacation rentals are closing for the season and I want to take advantage of off-season rates to smell the ocean one more time. Stores are attacking us with messages of harvest festivals and fall fashions, but I'm not ready to give up white capris just yet. While I love the fall season, there is a part of me that grieves the loss of sunshine. I know it won't be long before it's dark shortly after 5 PM. As I turn on my sunlamps inside, shorts and sandals are still calling me and I can feel the sand between my toes. I'm yearning for Indian Summer to create one last summer memory. And I ask myself, did I live summer fully or did I let it slip away? How about you? Have you embraced the seasons and experienced the gifts God has provided?

celebrate
SEPTEMBER

244. Dive into fall.

I don't know about you, but I need a ritual. Pull out the sweaters and pack up the summer items. Gather a bag of winter clothes you no longer wear and donate them to the Goodwill or other charity.

245. Celebrate Labor Day.

Whether it's with family and friends gathering around the BBQ grill or the pool, enjoy this last down day.

246. Camping.

Before old man winter arrives, take advantage of Indian summer and enjoy a last camp out.

247. Enjoy a Saturday Matinee. Go ahead. Eat the popcorn!

248. Celebrate Cheese Pizza Day.

249. Honor a teacher.
Kind words warm hearts. Think about someone you must thank for encouraging your child. Give them a "Thankful for You" gift.

250. Celebrate Oktoberfest.

251. Go apple picking.
Did you know 2,500 varieties of apples are grown in the United States, and 7,500 varieties of apples grown throughout the world? According to farmflavor.com America's favorite apple is the Gala apple. What's yours?

252. Celebrate National Teddy Bear Day.
On September 9, bring a few huggable stuffed animals to a children's hospital.

253. Celebrate National Grandparents Day.
This is a day to honor the elderly. If you don't have living grandparents, visit a nursing home and honor a few residents. President Jimmy Carter initiated this holiday back in 1978 and it always falls on the first Sunday after Labor Day.

254. Discover a Hot Air Balloon Festival. If you're brave, take a ride.

255. Participate in a Harvest Festival.

256. *journal it!*

Positive Thinking Day. Pick an aspect of your life that challenges you and make a list of 5 positive things about that situation.

257. Attend a Fall Music Festival.

258. Give a thank you gift –
to someone who will not expect it.

259. gratitude check

Think about the things you take for granted and how sad you would be to lose them. Make a list then take a few minutes to feel gratitude these things exist in your life. For instance, eyesight. We see every day, but don't think about how it would be if we lost our eyesight. Can you imagine being in the dark every day? I am grateful to see the colors, the beauty of nature, my family, my dog. Make your own list.

260. Indulge in an afternoon siesta nap.

Open the windows and left the fresh air bathe you as you snooze away and re-energize.

261. gratitude check

Gather your coworkers together for a "gratitude circle". Take turns telling each other what you are grateful for.

262. Fall forward and think about your goals.

What are three things you would begin if you weren't afraid. What's stopping you?

263. Send a Gratitude letter to someone who has impacted your life.

264. Invite a friend for a Pumpkin Spiced Latte at your favorite coffee shop.

265. Make someone's day amazing.

Look for opportunities to be generous.

266. Who's your hero?

Pick an everyday hero in your life and give them a thank you gift that says you appreciate them. A few ideas might be your child's teacher, bus driver, the door man, or the janitor.

267. gratitude check:

What is a talent or skill you have that you are grateful for? How can you share that with someone?

268. Visit a Pumpkin Patch and buy pumpkins to decorate your porch.

269. *journal it!*

What made you smile today? Make a list of 5 things to smile about.

270. Celebrate National Honey Month.
Purchase a jar of regional raw honey.

271. Enjoy a fall picnic at a local park. Collect leaves.

272. Take a shopping trip downtown.
Enjoy lunch from one of the local street vendors.

273. National Mulled Cider Day, September 30.
To make delicious mulled cider, all you need is a large pot, apple cider, brown sugar, nutmeg, allspice, orange slices, and lemon juice. Bring to a boil and stir. Pour in a cup, add a cinnamon stick and enjoy! For an alcoholic version, add rum.

GIVE *thanks* with a GRATEFUL *Heart*

appreciate your choice to be
THANKFUL

be thankful. It sounds a lot easier than it feels sometimes. It's easy to be thankful when everything seems perfect in our lives. The true benefits of gratitude come when we receive everything with a thankful heart.

Today think about things that concern you and displease you. What might be inviting fear into your heart? Step back and look for hidden blessings. Is the challenge leading you to grow into new open doors? Are relationship issues an opportunity to draw closer to someone?

I remember a time when I lost nearly all my material possessions. Quickly, I went from abundance to lack. Looking back, I am grateful because I learned these things are fleeting and unimportant. All material things are easily replaced. How many things do we hold on to thinking we just can't let that go? We wonder how we could ever live without cable, big screen TVs, or motorhomes.

True riches are in people; family and friends who stick with us no matter what. The people who love us in the little house or the sprawling mansion.

The friends willing to spend time with you when you no longer have the most comfortable surroundings or the jet ski.

What hardships have you faced that you now see as a blessing?

MEMORIES I AM GRATEFUL FOR...

MEMORIES I AM GRATEFUL FOR...

october

> **"Love is of all passions the strongest, for it attacks simultaneously the head, the heart and the senses."**
>
> LAO TZU

October is one of the best months to celebrate your senses; sight, touch, hearing, taste, and smell. Everything about October speaks of warmth. From the cozy sweaters and boots, to the vibrant colors, and sweet smelling hot apple cider. It's the month we don't want to be lazy. We move from lounging in the sunshine to the hustle and bustle of decorating with pumpkins and inviting loved ones into our homes for good food and conversation. We're raking leaves and jumping in them. What is your favorite fall memory?

celebrate OCTOBER

274. **Make a list of 4 things you can celebrate each week of October.**
Think about milestones in your life, victories and other successes.

275. **Plan a fall camping trip to one of the KOA Campgrounds.**

276. **Book a family fall photo shoot at a favorite outdoor location.**
If you can't hire a professional photographer, take turns taking
pictures of each other. Each photo will be a reminder of the fun you
had that day.

277. Celebrate the outdoors – improves focus and concentration.

Fresh air improves blood pressure and heart rate. It not only cleans your lungs but also your mind to give you more energy and making you feel happier. Even if you step outside for 15 minutes during the day. Take time to smell the roses.

278. Take a day trip!

Rent a car you would love to drive and take a day trip to enjoy the fall foliage.

279. National Smile Day is October 6.

Smiling not only produces hormones that boost your health by boosting your immune system and your mood but will affect those of whom you give a warm smile. Make a conscious effort to smile at everyone you meet today. Smiling is contagious. Note the chain reaction.

280. Celebrate simplicity.

Pick one thing that would simplify your life and do it.

281. Write a letter to tell someone what they mean to you.

282. Make homemade soup and bring a batch to a neighbor.

283. Volunteer at a retirement home.

Many elderly people have no family and days leading to the holidays can be the most depressing time for them. Bond a friendship.

284. Capture a fall sunrise.

285. Visit a corn maze.

286. Skype a family member.

287. *gratitude check:*

Make a list of 5 people who have inspired you and why this has made a difference in your life.

288. Do a Random Act of Kindness today.

289. Find a good joke and spread it around.
Laughter is good for the soul.

290. Plan a BFF fall getaway day or weekend.

291. Host a Harvest Party to celebrate fall.

292. Set aside a cooking day and make all your favorite foods.
Freeze food to enjoy throughout the month.

293. *gratitude check:*

Start a thankful jar and fill it until Thanksgiving Day. Take turns passing it around the family dinner table to share and recall the blessings of the year.

294. Pull out all your favorite fuzzy blankets and enjoy and evening around the firepit.

295. Visit a county fair and ride the Ferris Wheel.

296. Explore a nearby park and enjoy the beautiful fall colors.

297. Celebrate people.
Pick 5 people to give praise to today.

298. *journal it!*

Think about 5 senses that come alive during fall. Write down your happiest memories that involve taste, smell, hearing, touch, and sight you enjoy during the fall season.

299. *gratitude check:*

Think about 3 relationships that bring joy to your life. List the reasons for each one.

300. Let your inner child to emerge.
Get creative with Play Dough.

301. **Did you know that dark chocolate regulates cortisol, the stress hormone?**

Savor a piece of dark chocolate today with your favorite hot beverage.

302. **Visit a pumpkin patch and pick out pumpkins to decorate your front porch or entry.**

303. **It's all about pumpkins today. Make pumpkin Whoopie Pies.**

304. *journal it!*

Write about a childhood fall memory.

MEMORIES I AM GRATEFUL FOR ...

MEMORIES I AM GRATEFUL FOR ...

november

> "*Gratitude is the healthiest of all human emotions.*
> *The more you express gratitude for what you have,*
> *the more likely you will have even more*
> *to express gratitude for.*"
>
> **ZIG ZIGLAR**

Fall forward. Colder, shorter days, but oh how beautiful they are! I am grateful for this last month of fall tapestry! Colors, family-fun activities, and excitement are all around. We are getting ready to enter holiday season. This month we crank it into high gear and indulge in every scent, taste, and pleasure around us. The days of laziness are gone, and energy drives us like a car on the Indie 500. We're on the go!

Two of my favorite things this month are cozy sweaters and fall color pallets. If you love sweaters, boots, and scarves as much as I do, this is the month to enjoy them while it's not too cold, before the blistery winter exchanges the cuteness of fashion boots for heavy snow boots.

We enjoy inside activities. Decorating, cooking, and entertaining. Thanksgiving brings dear friends and family close as we enjoy all those things we are thankful for.

The month to cuddle up in your favorite sweats and binge watch your favorite movies with a mug of your favorite hot beverage. What fall beverage are you craving?

celebrate
NOVEMBER

305. **Make homemade hot chocolate and marshmallows.**
Enjoy a delicious hot cup with a friend or loved one this evening.

306. Select a couple Thanksgiving crafts to do this month.

Gather materials so you are ready to begin when time allows.

307. Choose a couple you'd like to know better and invite them to dinner.

308. *gratitude check:*

List 3 things you love about your life.

309. Volunteer your weekend to helping an elderly neighbor with their fall clean-up projects.

310. Think about three material blessings you have and how you can use them to bless someone else.

Plan who you can give them to this month.

311. Do a secret Act of Kindness today.

312. Make gratitude cards and send them to your friends and family.

313. Treat yourself to a signature fragrance.

314. Read Angela Duckworth's book, GRIT -

The Power of Passion and Perseverance

315. *journal it!*

Think about your talents and skills. List your top 5. Write about something you learned and the best teacher that taught you.

316. *gratitude check:*

Enjoy the little things. Make a list of 3 small things that make a huge difference in your life.

317. Celebrate authenticity.

You are one of a kind. Stop comparing yourself to others. Think of one thing that makes you unique. How can you share that?

318. *journal it!*

Write about a time when someone showed you kindness. How did you respond?

319. Be a blessing.

Think about your neighbor and pick a practical way you can serve them each week this season. Giving has a way of bouncing back to you.

320. Fall forward into new beginnings.

Opportunities result from where we are. Even a small change will create new beginnings. Where can you change your daily habits?

321. Buy a snack for a coworker and deliver it secretly.

No matter what, never let her know it was you.

322. *journal it!*

List 3 things you fear and what you can do to drop that worry. What steps could you take to overcome your fear?

323. Look for someone in your office that has no companion at lunch and get to know them.

Let your words bring encouragement to them.

324. Take a fall discovery walk and find things that show evidence of a changed season.

325. *gratitude check:*

List 3 challenging things in your life that have had positive outcomes.

326. Set your alarm to get up early tomorrow.

Those with an early morning ritual are more cheerful and productive throughout the day.

327 Take a fall road trip to enjoy the spectacular colorfest of this season.

328. Celebrate others by making a daily habit of serving someone each day.

Pick someone that does not live with you. Be purposeful in your decision. Whom can I serve today?

329. Enjoy a fall festival.

From music to art to food, there is something for every taste and passion.

330. Create a sleep ritual to prepare for the shorter days ahead.

Studies have shown those who prepare for sleep have a more restful sleep and are more productive during the day. Diming the lights one hour before bed will trigger your brain to start the sleep process.

331. Write a letter to your child.

332. Do something that scares you.

333. *journal it!*

Beauty is in the eye of the beholder. Describe the most beautiful thing you've ever seen.

334. Bake an apple pie from scratch.

335. Make a homemade pizza.

MEMORIES I AM GRATEFUL FOR ...

MEMORIES I AM GRATEFUL FOR ...

winter

> **the heavens declare thy glory of god,
> and the firmament sheweth his handiwork.
> day unto day uttereth speech,
> and night unto knowledge.
> there is no speech or language
> where their voice is not heard.**
>
> **PSALM 19:1-3**

I love winter. Growing up in upstate New York, we had TONS of snow! I always looked forward to this season of rest and healing. As you begin this season, enter its gates with a sense of wonder and thanksgiving. Begin each day with gratitude for what the day holds. No matter what you are facing, blessings are everywhere. If you have not already discovered them, they may be brewing just beneath the surface, but they are there. Some blessings are hidden in the corner begging to be found. Uncover them, and the light will shine on these heavenly gifts until they become the bright focal points of your day. Gratitude will release more blessings and lead to an overflowing life of abundance.

The Bible says that God inhabits the praises of His people. Thank Him for simple pleasures, for sunshine, snow that cleans the air, quiet moments, laughter, the coffee you're drinking, your abilities, the people you love, people you can bless. Be the answer to someone's prayer.

Open your heart to receive the small things as the richest blessings. The best things in life are free. A celebrated life is a lifestyle of gratitude and thanksgiving, season after season, day after day. Treat leisure as a gift of time. Don't waste them. Treasure five minutes between appointments, while standing in line at the post office. Make the most moments to connect and be a blessing to others.

As you wait for your coffee to perk, look out a nearby window and seize the awesomeness that lives in your own backyard. Trees glazed with ice in the morning sunlight, diamonds of ice shimmering on the blanket of snow covering the ground. What gifts do you see there?

Witness at least one sunrise this winter season and observe as God releases the gift of the day. I promise you; it may be a regular morning ritual if not already.

The most spectacular sunrise I saw was while at the North Rim of the Grand Canyon. I got up early to sit on the veranda of the lodge to catch a 5:30 AM sunrise. Knowing there would be other travelers heading there to claim their favorite spot, I got up at 4 AM. I knew this event would be a precious sight and couldn't wait to get there. With camera in hand, I quietly slipped out of the cabin as my family slumbered in their beds. I felt I'd be one of only a handful up this early. To my astonishment, dozens of people stood against the wall. Couples were already hiking down the trails in search of the perfect spot to receive this gift that The Lord was preparing for anyone who desired to see a glimpse of His handiwork. I can imagine Him in heaven excited by the crowds, getting ready to give a repeat show to many. Longing and loving the opportunity to bless His children with another one-of-a-kind, breathtaking view.

As the time drew near, the crowd grew and people from all nations, creeds, and colors stood in enthusiastic anticipation waiting for the ball of fire that would soon emerge to light the sky. I watched in awe as the sun slowly peaked above the edge of the canyon rim. Suddenly, time stood still, and all was quiet. Silence brings a sense of peace, and we all were awestruck by the majestic beauty and colors that exploded into the morning sky. We all soaked up the experience receiving this gift now, not only etched into our memory but seared into our hearts. At this moment, there was total harmony. This gift knew no skin color, language barrier, discrimination, or hatred. Each person stood humbly to receive the compelling whisper of God woven throughout the brilliant sky and hovering over the canyon rim to simply say; Be blessed. I love you.

All the stress and anxiety melted away from each soul that stood there to receive. In that peaceful moment, we felt God.

> *"Praise the Lord, O Jerusalem!*
> *Praise your God, O Zion.*
> *For He has strengthened the bars of your gates;*
> *He Has blessed your children within you.*
> *He makes peace in your borders,*
> *And fills you with the finest wheat.*
> *He sends out His command to the earth;*
> *His word runs very swiftly.*
> *He gives snow like wool;*
> *He scatters the frost like ashes;*
> *He casts out His hail like morsels;*
> *Who can stand before His cold?"*

PSALM 147: 12-17

december

> "*We make a living by what we get,*
> *but we make a life by what we give.*"
>
> WINSTON CHURCHILL

ECEMBER IS ALL ABOUT GIVING. BUT HOW OFTEN DO WE GET SO CAUGHT UP IN THE commercialism of Christmas we forget the true meaning of Christmas? Our gifts can never equal the gift of our Savior, but it's the symbolism behind our gifts that matter. Often, the best gift we can give this season is the gift of ourselves; our time. I learned from experience, giving time isn't unselfish. It seems this gift has a way of bouncing right back to us. As we give of ourselves, we the giver become a receiver.

To some, winter is harsh and place where all the fun stops, but really in the cycle of seasons, this is our time of healing. Think about animals in the wild. They hibernate. And likewise, God made this as a time for people to rest. As days become shorter, we are to ease into a slower pace, more sleep, a time to meditate. Leisurely moments with family and friends. Take time this month to soothe your soul, become a cheerful giver and celebrate your family and friends.

Do you ever feel like the holiday time just whizzed by? The most enjoyable holiday moments are after December 25 when I can enjoy my tree and the madness of shopping has gone into hibernation for yet another year. But what if we could enjoy the entire season without the stress? Imagine experiencing Christmas this year as it was appreciated during simpler times and celebrate this December with meaning and purpose.

celebrate
DECEMBER

336. Enjoy a horse drawn carriage ride.

337. Recognize each day this month as a personal gift to you.

Take time to embrace each day and savor something special. Laugh, play, and enjoy this seasons activity rather than getting caught up in to-do lists and overloaded schedules that take the fun out of this season.

338. Start a weekly or monthly family night to celebrate spending time with your loved ones.

Play games, watch movies, enjoy a special theme meal. Allow each member to help in planning this special celebration.

339. Let music stir your soul.

Plan a time to sit and enjoy your favorite Christmas songs while enjoying the tree. Serve your favorite hot beverage.

340. Celebrate nature.

Dress up your outdoor trees with strands of popcorn and birdseed ornaments. If you're feeling extraordinarily ambitious, you can make the birdseed ornaments.

341. Make Christmas ornaments to share with neighbors.

342. *gratitude check:*

List all the things in your life that make you feel content.

343. Expand your friendship circle.

Connect with one old friend and take the first step in starting a new friendship.

344. *journal it!*

Make a list of your holiday traditions and add one or two to the list.

345. Organize your old photos. Share them with family members.

346. Start a scrapbook project.

347. Make gift giving fun by playing games.

Send the recipients on a treasure hunt, gift swaps, and other activities to emphasize the giving and receiving more than the gift itself.

348. *gratitude check:*

Today is a day to be thankful to God's gifts to you. Think about 3 abilities you have that differ from others.

349. Participate in one of the holiday festivals in your town.

350. Bring a small gift to each of your co-workers.

A small sack of truffles, or other small treats and holiday items will be a welcome surprise.

351. Ask someone you'd like to know better to join you for coffee.

352. Buy a thank you gift for someone who helped you during the year.

353. Make homemade sugar scrubs and put in pretty jars with ribbon and give away as gifts.

Keep one for yourself!

354. If you're fortunate to have snow, build a snow fort.

355. Make snow angels in the snow.

356. Go sledding or snowmobiling.

357. *journal it!*

Write about your favorite childhood Christmas memory. Name that unforgettable gift you received.

358. Participate in a holiday food drive.

359. Celebrate the start of the Christmas season with a Victorian tree trimming gathering.

360. Create quarterly seasonal rituals.

Winter walks in the snow. Build a snowman. Celebrate the start of every season.

361. *gratitude check:*

Decorate a Gratitude Jar. Celebrate 3-5 things you are grateful for each day and put them on a slip of paper. During the month (and year if you keep going), you will have dozens of things to give thanks for.

362. Make and hand deliver holiday cards with a basket of goodies.

Don't treat the entire neighborhood but celebrate this season carefully choosing a few select people thank or someone who touched your heart this year.

363. Gather clothing to give to a local homeless shelter.

You can also donate to your local Salvation Army or Goodwill who will often pick up your donation.

364. Give the gift of time.

Fill holiday gift bags with hand lotions, lip balms, and other items, and visit a few residents of a nursing home. Many precious people receive no visitors throughout the season. The receptionist can tell you who needs a companion. Be a kind heart and a light to someone.

365. Celebrate God's creation.

Whether you're viewing a scene overlooking the Grand Canyon, the Fiji Islands, or a peaceful backyard, schedule at least one sunrise this month to experience God pulling the shades open and celebrate the gift of a new day.

appreciate the gift of
GIVING

They say it is better to give than receive. I suppose the reason behind in giving a gift, you also give to yourself. According to the Greater Good Science Center at UC at Berkeley, giving makes us feel happier than if we spent money buying something for ourselves. Generosity leads to better health. Studies have proven that seniors who volunteer and give their time enjoy better health and longevity likely because giving reduces stress. Giving also improves social connections, generates gratitude, and is highly contagious. This is one bug you want to go viral this winter!

> *"So, let each one give as he purposes in his heart, not grudgingly or of necessity; for God loves a cheerful giver."*
>
> **2 CORINTHIANS 9:7**

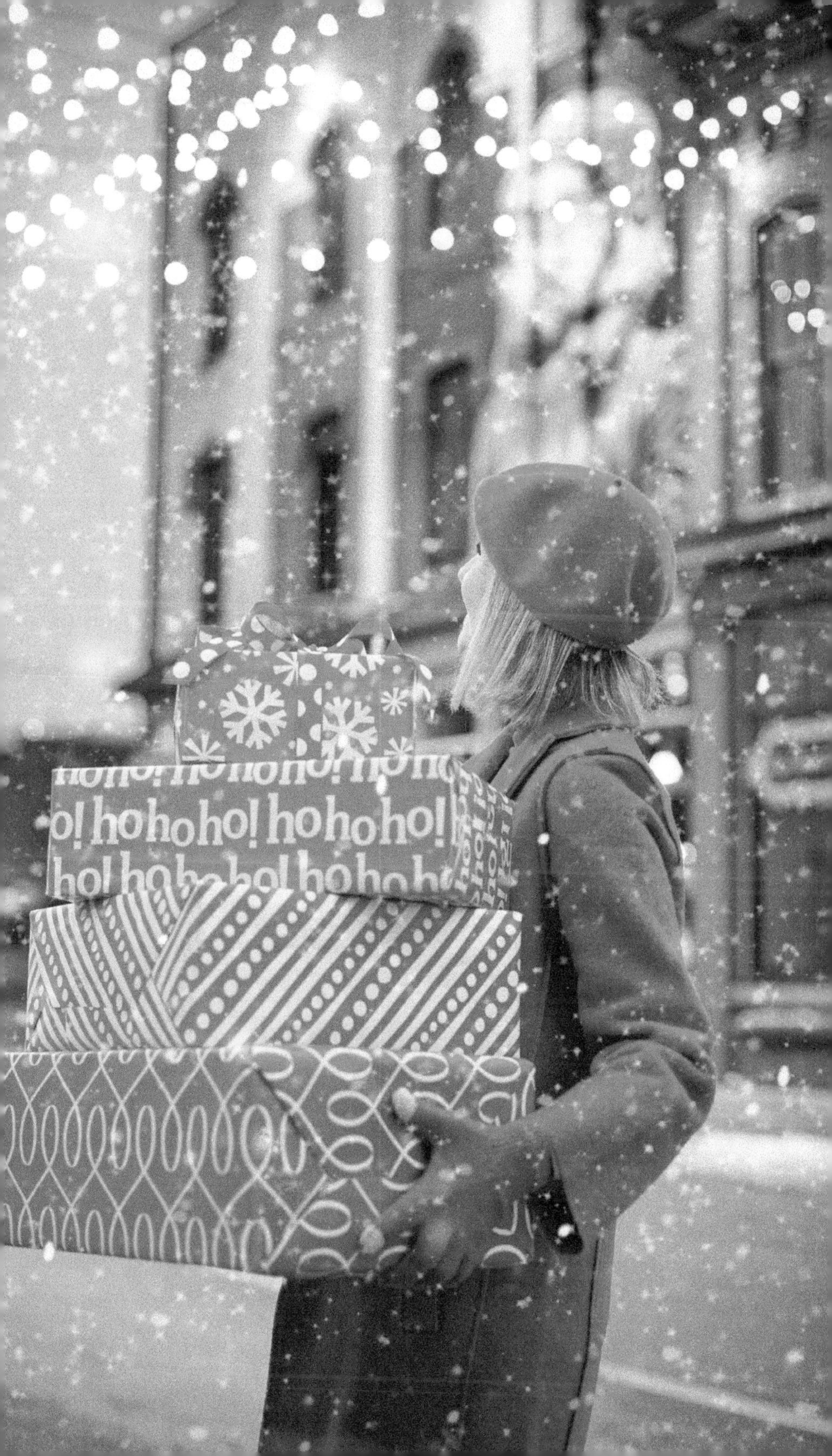
hohoho! hohoho!

MEMORIES I AM GRATEFUL FOR...

MEMORIES I AM GRATEFUL FOR...

"

> "*I will praise You, O Lord, with my whole heart,*
> *I will tell of all Your marvelous works.*
> *I will be glad and rejoice in You;*
> *I will sing praise to Your name, O Most High*"

PSALM 9:1-2

about the author

*d*iana LéGere is a Christian writer whose passion is to share her faith and life experiences through her words, and help other women do the same.

As the founder of a women's writing group, Women of Words, she works with first-time authors to provide editing, ghostwriting, and coaching services to help new authors get their books published.

Diana has written professionally for two decades as a journalist, columnist, and copywriter. She is the author of four books, including the cookbook Feeding Families Authentic Southern: History, Traditions & Stories, the memoir journal Ripples: A Memoir of Reflection, Celebrations of Praise: 365 Ways to Fill Each Day with Meaningful Moments, and the upcoming memoir journal, He Spoke: A Memoir of Grace.

A New York native, Diana now lives in central Virginia. She is mother to three children and has two grandchildren. When not writing, she enjoys music, photography, painting, and bird watching. She can also be known to binge watch an entire season of the Mary Tyler Moore Show and loves classic old movies.

make TODAY amazing

BOOKS BY DIANA LÉGERE

Celebrations of Praise:
365 Ways to Fill Each Day with Meaningful Moments

Ripples: A Memoir of Reflection

Authentic Southern: Recipes, Traditions & Stories

**Books are available online through Amazon and
Barnes & Noble**

**If you've enjoyed this book,
please post a review on Goodreads and Amazon**

Coming soon!

He Spoke: A Memoir of Grace

recipe

DIANA'S FAVORITE GUMBO

1/3 cup Extra-Virgin olive oil
3 boneless chicken breasts, cubed
3 turkey sausages, sliced (substitute Andouille sausage if preferred)
1 lb medium shrimp, shelled and deveined
1 large yellow onion, chopped
1 large red pepper, chopped
2 cloves garlic, minced
1 (14.5 ounce) can diced tomatoes
4 cups chicken bone broth
2 bay leaves
Handful chopped Italian parsley
Salt and pepper to taste
Cooked Jasmine rice

In a Dutch oven, heat olive oil and sauté boneless breast and sausages with onion, pepper and garlic until browned. Add can of tomatoes and chicken stock and simmer for 30 minutes. Add water if broth thickens. Serve over a bowl of jasmine rice.

Note: This is not a traditional New Orlean's Gumbo. It is a delicious comfort food that will warm you up in the cold of the winter.

bonus activities

JOURNAL PROMPTS

--What would you do if you knew you couldn't fail?

--If time were not an issue, what would you add to your daily routine?

--Recall a time when a loved one celebrated you.

--Describe a time when you were faced with a difficult choice.

--Describe the perfect day.

GRATITUDE CHECK

--List a difficult time you experienced that you are now thankful for.

--Think of something you aren't happy about. Now, list 3 things you are grateful for in THAT situation.

--Write about something you are grateful not to have experienced and why.

--Name a simple activity you are grateful for that you might otherwise take for granted.

--List 3 sounds that you couldn't live without.

MEANINGFUL MOMENTS ACTIVITY

This section is for you. Each time you have a simple memorable moment, write it here.

Write to me and let me know about your MEANINGFUL MOMENTS!
Email: womenofwords.rva@gmail.com

meaningful moments

meaningful moments